The Willowisp Book Of JEWISH HOLIDAYS

by Karla Dougherty

illustrations by David Schulz

with special thanks to Rabbi Kenneth Bromberg

To my mother, Irma Ramm Rosenberg

Published by Willowisp Press, Inc.
10100 SBF Drive, Pinellas Park, Florida 34666

Copyright © 1992 Willowisp Press, Inc.

Printed in the United States of America

2 4 6 8 10 9 7 5 3 1

ISBN 0-87406-639-5

Contents

The Jewish Year

Jewish people live in many different countries all over the world. There are Jews in the United States and Canada, Europe, the Russian Federation, and in the countries of the Middle East, including Israel, the Jewish homeland. And wherever they live, Jewish people follow many of the customs of their countries. American Jews speak English and celebrate the Fourth of July. Italian Jews speak Italian and eat a diet rich in pasta.

But no matter where they live, Jewish people also follow some of the oldest and most beautiful traditions in the world. Jews everywhere are connected by their love and respect for the ancient Jewish customs they follow, especially at holiday times. Over the thousands of years that Jews have been a people, they have worshipped God in the same ways, speaking the same Hebrew words, and performing the same actions that their ancestors used in the deserts of the Holy Land so long ago.

This Willowisp book will help you understand the meaning and see the beauty of the many holiday celebrations of the Jewish year.

Chag Sameach!

Rosh Hashanah

Everyone knows when it's New Year's Eve, right? It's December 31, the night when it is customary to wear silly hats, watch the ball come down on TV, and stay up until midnight. But Jewish boys and girls get to help their families celebrate another new year. It's the holiday of Rosh Hashanah, which means "the beginning of the year" in Hebrew.

The Jewish year has its own calendar, and it begins with this holiday. Rosh Hashanah celebrates the birth of the world, when God created the earth, moon, stars, sun, and man. The Jewish new year begins in the fall, in September or October.

Jews believe that on this day, God takes down a big book called the Book of Life and in it writes the names of everyone. Then He decides who will have a good year. Because God knows that no one is perfect, He gives everyone a second chance to make up for his or her mistakes. In the synagogue, Jews say to each other, "May you be written down for a good year in the Book of Life."

Rosh Hashanah usually begins with a fancy meal. You would have different things in different countries, but one thing is always the same: For a sweet and productive new year, Jews everywhere eat apple slices dipped in honey before the meal begins. (The honey stands for the sweet, and the apples stand for the productive.)

But before long, a strange, loud sound is heard: *T'akkunnah! Tutututakana! Tekiahhh!* It's the sound of the *shofar*, an ancient musical instrument made from the curved horn of a ram. For thousands of years it has called Jews to their place of worship, the synagogue. And tonight, on Rosh Hashanah, it's calling you, too.

The shofar's sounds are so loud that Jews believe it reaches God's ears, so He will know to listen for their prayers. Joshua had his men blow shofars as they marched around the walls of Jericho—and you may recall how quickly those walls came tumbling down! Now Jews sound the shofar only on the high holy days, which begin with Rosh Hashanah.

Here is a prayer to say on Rosh Hashanah:

Remember us for life
King, who delights in life,
And inscribe us
In the book of life.

Challah

Challah is a favorite food during the Rosh Hashanah feast. You can make this thick, crusty bread in special shapes for the holiday. On Rosh Hashanah, the bread is round to symbolize the hope for a full new year. Sometimes it's made with raisins so that your year will always be sweet.

Other Rosh Hashanah decorations for challah are ladders, which show that your good deeds are going up into heaven, wings to help your prayers and wishes get up to heaven faster, and crowns, symbols of God. You can make your own challah decorations in special shapes. But you'll need to use the oven, so make sure an adult is around in case you need help. Here's how:

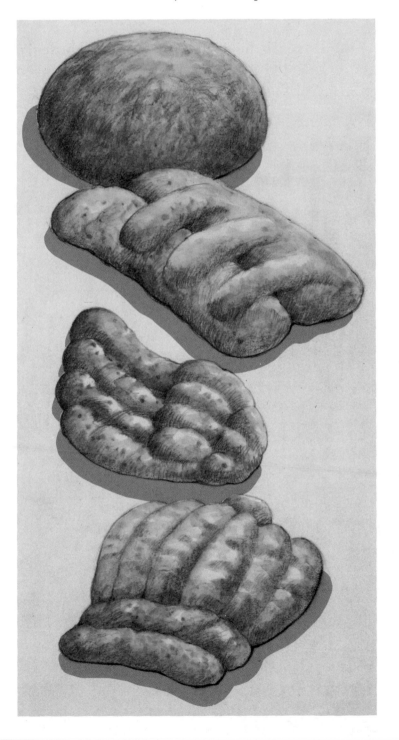

1. Open a package of store-bought, refrigerated biscuit dough. Save the instructions on the package for oven temperature and baking time. Instead of separating the biscuits, roll the dough into one big ball.

2. Work the dough like clay and shape it into small ladders, wings, and crowns. Pinch pieces of dough together with your fingers. Use a fork to make wavy lines in the dough.

3. Put food coloring into four bowls. With a paint brush that has never been used, paint your shapes with the red, blue, green, and yellow food coloring.

4. Add sprinkles, colored sugar, redhots, or jelly beans to your creations.

5. Put your dough shapes on a cookie sheet, but leave plenty of room between them because they'll expand when they bake. Follow the instructions on the biscuit package you saved.

6. In a few minutes you'll have lots of delicious challah shapes to eat, decorate the round loaf with, or give as presents to your family and friends.

Rosh Hashanah Cards

Make your own Rosh Hashanah cards and send them to friends and family. It's a way of saying hello and wishing that their new year will be sweet.

1. Cut a piece of construction paper in half. Fold it in the middle so that it will open like a card.

2. On the front of the card, draw a shofar, a crown, an apple, or a round challah.

3. Above your design on the front write these Hebrew words: *Leshana Tova Tikatevu*. They mean "May you be written down for a good year." You might want to try practicing writing this before you write it on your card.

4. Inside the card, write "Happy New Year." Don't forget to sign your name!

Tashlich

In ancient times, Jews believed that the sea could wash away their sins, so they cleansed themselves in the water. This is called *tashlich*. Today, many Jews repeat this ritual symbolically as part of their Rosh Hashanah holiday. They put bread crumbs in their pockets and go to a river, stream, or lake. They turn open their pockets and let the bread crumbs drop into the water. They say, "Send our sins to the depths of the sea."

Yom Kippur

Yom Kippur, the Day of Atonement, is the holiest of all the Jewish holidays. It comes 10 days after Rosh Hashanah, so it is celebrated in the fall, too. This is the day you fast—you can't eat breakfast, lunch, or a snack until the sun goes down on this special day. You can't even have a glass of water!

Atonement means forgiveness, and Yom Kippur is the day when Jews ask each other to forgive the wrongs they have done during the year. By fasting and going to the synagogue, Jews ask God for forgiveness and promise to do better in the coming year. At the synagogue, you'll hear this well-known story of forgiveness:

Long ago, God told a man named Jonah to go to the evil city of Nineveh. He was to tell the people there that unless they changed their ways, God would destroy them. Jonah was a very holy man, and he didn't want to give the wicked people of Nineveh a second chance. He felt that God should destroy them right away. So instead of obeying God, Jonah tried to run away from his duty. He got on a ship, but God found him and sent a terrible storm. Huge waves crashed and rolled. Jonah fell overboard and was swallowed whole by a whale.

Jonah was very frightened in the belly of the whale. He finally realized that he could not run away from God. He also realized that everybody deserves a second chance—even the wicked people of Nineveh.

Jonah prayed and asked God for forgiveness. God heard him and commanded the whale to cough Jonah up onto the shore. Then Jonah went to Nineveh and delivered the message. He told the people that they had one last chance to change their evil ways. And the people listened to Jonah. They became known as the good people of Nineveh from that time on.

Before you go to the synagogue, your parents may bless you with this special blessing: "May God bless you and protect you. May God shine His face upon you and be gracious to you. May God look kindly on you and grant you peace."

Everyone dresses up to go to the synagogue on Yom Kippur. But because Yom Kippur is the highest holy day, the rabbi and the cantor, who sings the special Yom Kippur prayers, will dress all in white as a sign of purity and holiness. They wear white robes and white *yarmulkes*, small

skullcaps, on their heads, and even white shoes and socks.

When the story of Jonah and the whale has been told, and the prayers of forgiveness and hope have been read, the shofar sounds one more time. Three stars appear in the darkening sky and the Day of Atonement is officially over. Everyone leaves the synagogue and it's time to go home and eat—at last!

A "Break the Fast" Meal You Can Make

Here's a "break the fast" meal you can make for your family when you come home from the synagogue.

1. Pour cold orange juice into tall glasses. Put a fresh strawberry and a sprig of mint on the rim of each glass for an extra special touch.

2. Ask an adult to slice enough bagels for everyone in your family. Put a wedge of softened cream cheese in two separate bowls. To one bowl add three pieces of lox (you can buy lox at the deli counter of the supermarket). With a fork, mash the lox into the cream cheese. Spread this mixture on half of your bagels. To the cream cheese in the other bowl, add two tablespoons of chives and a dash of garlic powder and onion powder. Mix this together with a spoon and spread it on the rest of the bagel halves. Put the bagel halves around the edges of a big platter. In the middle, place parsley, lettuce, and cherry tomatoes.

3. Toast slices of any kind of bread. While the bread is toasting, mix together a quarter cup of sugar and a quarter cup of cinnamon. Butter each slice of toast. Then, using a small spoon, sprinkle the mixture on each slice. Make eyes, a nose, and a smiling face. This treat will get your new year off to a sweet start!

The Sh'ma

The *Sh'ma* is the holiest of all Jewish prayers. Jews all over the world say this ancient prayer several times during a holiday service. When Jewish people say the Sh'ma, it connects them to their past. It connects them to the first Jews, wandering in the desert of long ago.

Sh'ma Yisrael Adonai Eloneynu Adonai Echad
Baruch Shem K'vod Malchuto L'olam Va'ed.

Hear, O Israel, the Lord is our God, the Lord is one.
Blessed be His name whose glorious kingdom is forever and ever.

Sukkot

Let the heavens rejoice, let the earth be glad, let the seas roar and the fields exult, then shall the trees of the forest sing for joy.

This psalm describes the delight and appreciation Jews feel on Sukkot, the harvest festival. It's a time when God asks Jews to be happy!

For thousands of years, Jews have celebrated Sukkot. In ancient Jerusalem, people came from many miles away for the festivities. They brought with them fat oxen and plump sheep, pigeons, sacks of flour, and clay jugs of wine.

In the morning and afternoon, there were prayers of thanksgiving for the rich harvest, and animal sacrifices to God. But the night was a time for dancing. Giant gold *menorahs*, or candelabra, were built especially for Sukkot. They had four branches. At the end of each branch was a cup filled with olive oil. When it got dark, the cups were lit, sending red flames into the air. Then everyone would dance in the candlelight until dawn.

Today Jews no longer have the giant menorahs for celebrating Sukkot. But they do build *sukkot*, booth-like open-air tents that their ancestors lived in while they roamed through the desert searching for the Promised Land. The holiday is named after these tents, which the ancient Jews named after the first oasis they came to in their wandering.

Starting four days after Yom Kippur, a serious and solemn holiday, Jews everywhere build sukkot. Maybe your community builds a big *sukkah* in a public place where everyone can enjoy it. Or maybe you and your family make a sukkah in your backyard. No matter where it is, a sukkah is made of wood, with bunches of fruits, vegetables, and branches hanging from the ceiling. The ceiling is made of wooden slats so that people inside can see the stars above. Sometimes the walls are covered with strings of cranberry or brightly colored paper chains.

The only furniture your sukkah needs is a table and some chairs. You can use a hollowed-out pumpkin as the centerpiece of your table, filling it with fruits and nuts. You and your friends and family can sit in the sukkah and watch the stars twinkling overhead. You can smell the tree branches and dirt. You can nibble on the fruits and nuts in your sukkah. And you can thank God for your wonderful friends and family, like your ancestors did so long ago.

Sukkot, Plain and Fancy

Sukkot come in all different shapes and sizes. Some are simple and homemade. Some are almost like little palaces. The most beautiful sukkah of all is in Jerusalem's Israel Museum. Made in Germany in the 1800s, this sukkah is made of many panels of wood. When the panels are stood up and put together in the right order, they not only make the walls of the sukkah, but they are also gorgeous hand-painted murals showing stories from the Bible.

If you're not very handy, you can buy a sukkah kit in specialty stores, with step-by-step instructions on how to put it together. Maybe the most unusual sukkah is the sukkah mobile, which is exactly what it sounds like! Jews in large cities make portable sukkot, putting them on the back of a truck. They take the sukkot around to hospitals, schools, and nursing homes, so people who can't build a sukkah can visit a sukkah that comes to them!

Sukkot Symbols

The *etrog* and the *lulav* are symbols of Sukkot. They represent the life-sustaining harvest. The etrog is a citrus fruit that grows in the Middle East and looks like a lemon. It keeps its fragrant smell for all seven days of Sukkot. The lulav is a palm branch that represents the strength, beauty, and goodness of the earth. When you go to the synagogue during Sukkot, you'll see the rabbi and others shake the lulav and the etrog several times during the service.

A Dollhouse Sukkah

You can make a miniature sukkah with a shoe box, scissors, some scrap material and construction paper, glue, crayons, pens or paint, and some old magazines. Here's how:

1. Take off the lid from the shoe box and put it aside. To make a door, cut out a square from the middle of the long side of the box. Paint or color the outside of the box to look like wood. Let the box dry if you used paint.

2. Glue a piece of scrap material over the door to look like a curtain.

3. Decorate the inside of the shoe box with tiny pictures of fruits and vegetables from the magazines, or draw your own. Glue them to the wall. Paint the floor to look like dirt.

4. Make a table with construction paper. You can make chairs from a toilet paper tube and construction paper. Cut the tube in short pieces. Draw seat cushions on the construction paper and cut them out. Glue the cushions to the pieces of tube. Paint them.

5. Look through the magazines to find a tiny picture of a lemon and a tree branch to be your etrog and lulav. Put them on the table.

6. Cut the lid of the shoe box into strips. Glue these strips across the top of the shoe box (so people can look inside your sukkah). Glue some grass or twigs across the top strips. Cut out or draw apples, peppers, or other fruits and vegetables. Dangle them from the roof with thread.

Hanukkah

Once upon a time, an evil king named Antiochus ruled much of the ancient Middle East. But Antiochus was greedy for more land. And he knew he could find money to hire more soldiers to build up his army if he went to Jerusalem, the capital of Judea. There, in the gold and marble temple of the Jews, he knew he could find riches and treasure.

But Antiochus wanted more than the Jews' treasure. He wanted to rule them, and he wanted them to worship his gods. When the Jews refused to worship his gods, Antiochus destroyed the temple in Jerusalem. He smeared dirt all over the temple, and brought pigs inside it to live. And he smashed containers that held holy oil, which kept the eternal light aflame.

But the Jews fought back. They used the hills and caves outside of Jerusalem for their base. Their leader, Judas, was very brave and taught his followers to fight bravely. They hit the enemy with swift attacks like hammer blows. Soon the fighters came to be known as the "Maccabees," the Hebrew word for hammer.

After three long years of fighting, the Maccabees finally drove Antiochus from their land. But they still faced one enormous task. Their temple, their holiest place, was in shambles. Many wondered if they could ever use it again for worship. But the Jews started to clean up the temple. They polished the golden gates and painted the walls. They swept and scrubbed. Finally, there was only one more thing to be done before the Jews could pray again in their temple: They had to light the eternal light with holy oil. The eternal light was held in a menorah, or candelabrum, in the temple courtyard. But Antiochus' soldiers had destroyed all the containers of holy oil except one. The priests needed eight days to make regular oil holy—but they had only enough oil for one day.

Judas Maccabeus lit the menorah anyway, even though he knew there wasn't enough oil. And a miracle happened! The oil in the menorah lasted for eight days, long enough for the priests to make more holy oil. At that moment, the holiday of Hanukkah was born.

Today, when Jews light the Hanukkah candles in their family menorah, they are celebrating the victory of Judas and the Maccabees over their enemy. And by lighting first one candle, then a second, and so on for the eight days of the holiday, Jews remember the miracle of the one small container of holy oil.

Hanukkah usually falls in December. Because it is such a joyous time, Jews give gifts to their family and friends. Sometimes they receive Hanukkah *gelt*, which means *money* in Yiddish, the old language of

Eastern European Jews. Sometimes they exchange small gifts on every one of the eight nights.

Jewish children also play with *dreidls* during Hanukkah. These little spinning tops were first used to trick the soldiers of Antiochus. He had ordered that Jewish children couldn't study their religion. But they did, anyway. And when the soldiers came around, the children hid their books and took out their dreidls to fool them!

One of the special foods for Hanukkah is *latkes*, or potato pancakes, with sour cream and applesauce. They're made with chopped-up potatoes, onions, and salt, and fried in oil, which commemorates the holy oil of Hanukkah.

Jews light the Hanukkah candles and sing Hanukkah songs. They open presents and play dreidl games. They think of the miracle of the holy oil on the first Hanukkah.

The Dreidl Game

Here are the four Hebrew letters that appear on the sides of the dreidl:

Nun   Heh   Gimmel   Shin

They stand for Hebrew words that mean "A great miracle happened there," referring to the victory over Antiochus and the miracle of the holy oil. In Israel, children use dreidls with letters that stand for "A great miracle happened *here*," because Israel is where the events of Hanukkah took place.

In one Dreidl game, each word is worth a certain number of points. *Gimmel* is worth 3, *heh* is worth 5, *nun* is worth 50, and *shin* is worth 300. The person who spins the highest letter gets to start the game. Then everyone takes turns spinning the dreidl. The first player who spins 1000 points wins the game.

Hanukkah Gifts You Can Make

Here are some ideas for Hanukkah gifts you can make for your family and friends.

1. Decorate brown paper lunch bags with gold stars, and pictures of dreidls, latkes, Maccabee swords, and gift-wrapped packages. Use crayons, markers, stickers, or pictures from magazines. Put nuts, raisins, jelly beans, or candy in each bag. Get some blue and white yarn (the colors of the flag of Israel) and twist the pieces together. Tie the yarn around the top of the bag and you've got a pretty package.

2. Make your own Hanukkah gelt. Buy a few plain chocolate bars and put them in the refrigerator until they're very cold. Using a cookie cutter, cut circles from the chocolate. Wrap each circle in a piece of aluminum foil—you've now got some money you can eat!

3. Your parents might especially like gift certificates—for things you promise to do! Cut a sheet of 8½ by 11-inch white construction paper into three triangles. Decorate the edges with stars, dreidls, blue stripes, and other designs. On the gift certificates you can write things like:

• I will give my parents a hug whenever they want one.

• I will wash and dry the dinner dishes for two weeks.

• I will clean up my room and make my bed every day this week.

• I will walk the dog when I come home from school every day for a month.

Dreidl Song

Here are the words and music to "The Dreidl Song," a favorite at Hanukkah:

I had a little dreidl, I made it out of clay.
And when it's dry and ready, oh dreidl, I shall play.
(chorus)
Oh dreidl, dreidl, dreidl, I made it out of clay,
And when it's dry and ready, oh dreidl, I shall play.

It has a lovely body, its leg's so short and thin.
And when it gets all tired, it drops and then I win.
(chorus)
Oh dreidl, dreidl, dreidl, its leg's so short and thin.
And when it gets all tired, it drops and then I win.

My dreidl's always playful, it loves to dance and spin.
A happy little dreidl. Come play, now let's begin!
(chorus)
Oh dreidl, dreidl, dreidl, it loves to dance and spin.
A happy little dreidl. Come play, now let's begin!

Purim

Bang the drums! Shake and rattle the noisemakers! Shout and stamp your feet! It's early spring, and time for Purim, the happiest and maybe the loudest holiday ever! Purim is the holiday that teaches us that we should never give up hope. At Purim, the rabbi takes out the scroll called the *Megillah* and reads the story of the brave and beautiful Queen Esther and how she saved the Jews from the evil Haman.

Long ago in Persia, the great King Ahasuerus wanted to find a new wife. But no women could move his heart until he saw Esther, the cousin of his royal letter-writer, Mordecai. But the king did not know she was Jewish. Mordecai told her to keep it a secret. He told her she might someday be able to help her people when she became queen.

But even the wise Mordecai didn't know how much help Esther would be. The king's powerful chancellor was a man named Haman. He was an Amalekite, a long-standing enemy of the Hebrew people. Haman wanted everyone at the court to bow down to him. But Mordecai refused. And the more he refused, the angrier Haman became. Finally he went to King Ahasuerus. He told him he had a plan to get rid of the kingdom's greatest enemy—and he would pay for the slaughter himself! Haman was very sly. He got the king to agree to his plan. But Haman didn't tell the king *who* the enemy was!

Haman's strategy to slay all Jews began with a game of chance. To find out the best time to launch his murderous plan, he cast lots using smooth stones—an ancient method that is a little like drawing straws or flipping a coin. In fact, *purim* means casting lots in Hebrew. The stones said that Haman should begin his slaughter the sooner the better, in early spring.

But Mordecai heard about the plot. He went to Queen Esther and told her that she was the only one who could save the Jews. She agreed to go to King Ahasuerus that night, even though he had not asked her to come. And to visit the king without an invitation meant death! The queen put on her most beautiful silk robe. She brushed her hair. She took a deep breath and walked through the palace corridor to the king. Luckily for Esther—and the Jewish people—the king truly loved her and was glad to see her. She told him her secret, that she was Jewish. And she told him about Haman's plot to murder all the Jews. Ahasuerus was so angry when he heard about the trick Haman had played on him that he had Haman hanged immediately! From that time on, the Jews of Persia lived in peace and safety. Esther had saved her people.

So that's why every time Jews hear Haman's name read in the Megillah, they twist and shake *graggers*, or noisemakers. They shout and boo to drown out his name. Because his name is mentioned 50 times in the reading, that's a lot of noise!

There's plenty of fun after the service too. Many synagogues have a tradition of acting out the Purim story called a *Purimspiel.* Other synagogues have carnivals. But more than anything else, Purim fun means dressing up, just like Halloween. You can dress up like the beautiful, brave Queen Esther or the evil Haman. You can be King Ahasuerus or wise Mordecai. Or you can dress up like a *hamantashen,* a triangular cookie made at Purim. Some say that the cookie looks like Haman's hat, or his foot, or even his ears!

Calling All Costumes!

Purim means dressing up like the characters from the story. Use your imagination!
Dressing up like Esther is easy. Borrow a nightgown and scarf from your mom. Wear the nightgown over a leotard and tights. Add a fancy belt. Use the scarf as a headdress. Keep it in place with bobby pins. Make a crown out of cardboard and aluminum foil. Wear it on top of your headdress. Add sandals, some lipstick and eye shadow, and you're all set.

Maybe Haman is more your style. Wrap a sheet around your bathing suit, tucking it in to make sure your suit doesn't show. Add a leather belt and sandals. Use a towel or sheet as a headdress, with a headband to keep it in place. Make a beard or buy a Halloween one and stick it on your chin. Make your eyebrows bushy with an eyebrow pencil. Add wrinkles and lines with the eyebrow pencil and white powder for a ghostly look.

Hamantashen

Bake your own hamantashen. (Make sure you have permission to use the oven and that there's an adult around in case you need help.) You'll need:

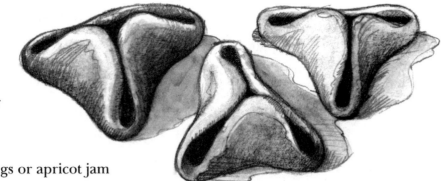

2 eggs

½ cup of vegetable oil

⅔ cup of sugar

1 tsp. of vanilla

1½ tsp. of baking powder

¼ tsp. of salt

2½ cups of flour

prune or poppy seed fillings or apricot jam

1. Preheat the oven to 350 degrees.

2. Put the eggs in a big bowl and beat them with an electric mixer until smooth.

3. Add the oil, sugar, vanilla, baking powder, and salt. Beat again until smooth.

4. Slowly add the flour. Mix until smooth. Wash your hands, then use them to push and pull the dough until it's smooth.

5. Using a rolling pin, roll out the dough on a flat surface.

6. Push the top of a glass into the dough, making circles. Cut away the rest of the dough, leaving the circles. Re-roll the leftover dough and make more!

7. Put a spoonful of filling in the center of each circle. Make a small triangle by pinching together two sides of the filled circle.

8. Place your triangles on a greased cookie sheet. Bake until your hamantashen are golden brown, about 30 minutes.

Make Your Own Gragger

It's simple to make your own gragger. Find a handful of small pebbles and two plastic cups. Put the pebbles in one of the cups, then staple or tape the two cups together. You can decorate the cups with stickers, pictures from magazines, colored paper, or your own drawings.

Passover

Tonight, the smells of simmering chicken soup and *knaidlach*, potato dumplings, fill the air. The dining room table looks beautiful, with a crisp white tablecloth, polished silver, and crystal wine glasses reflecting the flames of the flickering candles. The side table is piled high with bowls of fruit and macaroon cookies. There are enough places set at the table for your family, grandparents, and aunts, uncles, and cousins. Everyone is excited.

This is Passover, the night that's different from all the others. It's the night that Jews all over the world eat the special *seder* meal and remember their ancestors' escape from slavery in Egypt.

But before you can eat, it's time to hear the story of Passover—the story of how Moses, with God's help, led the children of Israel from slavery in Egypt to freedom in the Promised Land.

You'll hear how God sent plagues—terrible illnesses and other life-threatening problems—to the Egyptians. Some of the plagues included boils, locusts, lice, frogs, and more. But still the pharaoh would not let the Hebrews go free. Finally, God had to send the tenth and most terrible plague. The Angel of Death would come down and kill the firstborn child in each Egyptian house, including the pharaoh's own son.

But God told the Jews to sacrifice a lamb and smear some lamb's blood on the doors of their houses. This way, the Angel of Death would know which houses to spare, or pass over. And that's how this holiday got its name.

The Hebrews wandered in the desert for many years until they reached the Promised Land. And after all the stories, you probably feel like you've been waiting at least that long to eat! By now you can't wait to dive into the *gefilte* fish, the potato *kugel*, the sponge cake with strawberries, and the other foods.

Let's look at the table a little more closely. Next to the head of the table is a decorated *matzah* cover. It holds three pieces of matzah, the flat hard bread the fleeing Jews had to eat in the desert because they didn't have time to use yeast and wait for their bread to rise. The middle piece of matzah is special. It's the *afikomen*. Your father will hide it somewhere in the house and whoever finds it, gets a prize. Not all the matzah is covered with the decorated cloth. There are other plates of matzah on the table for everyone to eat. In fact, for the next eight days, you'll be eating a lot of matzah—for instance, matzah instead of toast for breakfast. Jews don't eat regular, yeasted bread, or *chometz*, at any time during Passover.

In the center of the table is the seder plate. On it you'll find a roasted bone to symbolize the lamb your ancestors sacrificed to God when they left Egypt. Next to the bone is a hard-boiled egg, to symbolize the heartiness of the ancient Jews. The *maror*, a bitter herb such as horseradish, represents the bitterness of slavery. The *charoset*, a mixture of fruit, cinnamon, nuts, and wine, symbolizes the bricks and mortar that the ancient Hebrews were forced to use to build the pharaoh's cities. Finally, there's a piece of green parsley, the *karpas*, which represents the coming spring, and the joy and hope of freedom.

It's a fantastic meal, but even at the end of it, there's more ritual. It's time to greet Elijah, an important, ancient prophet who is said to come to each seder. Your family has even left a glass of wine for him.

Make Your Own Charoset

To make charoset for your seder, you'll need:

2 apples, cored, peeled, and chopped

1/4 cup of sweet red Passover wine or grape juice

1/4 tsp. of cinnamon

1/2 cup of chopped nuts

1. Mix the apples with the wine or grape juice.

2. Add the cinnamon and stir with a fork.

3. Add the walnuts and continue to stir the mixture.

4. Store the mixture covered in the refrigerator until the seder.

The Four Questions

It's a Jewish tradition that the youngest child at the table asks traditional questions about Passover. Maybe that's you! Everyone sings or recites the traditional answers. Those questions and answers are:

Why on this night do we eat only matzah?

The matzah reminds us of the bread our ancestors ate in the desert.

Why on this night do we eat only bitter herbs?

The bitter herbs remind us of the bitterness of slavery.

On all other nights, we do not even dip once. Why on this night do we dip twice?

Dipping our karpas in salt water symbolically turns the Jews' tears of slavery into the joy of freedom. Dipping our maror into the charoset symbolically flavors the bitterness of slavery with the sweetness of God's rescue. The bitter with the sweet reminds us that joy and sadness are often linked together—that many experiences in life are bittersweet.

Why on this night do we recline while eating?

We recline at the seder because in ancient times free men ate from a reclining position on small sofas.

The Haggadah

The seder has been celebrated the same way for centuries. It's done the same way all over the world—the United States, England, France, the Russian Federation, Canada, and elsewhere. Jews everywhere follow the procedures in a book called the *Haggadah*. Each person at the table gets a copy of the book. Some Haggadahs are very beautiful and elaborate, with gold and jewels. Most of them are less fancy, though. All explain what is happening in the service, step by step.

To help make your seder table beautiful, make your own Haggadah book covers. Take a sheet of construction paper and trace one of the prayer books on it. Make sure there's enough space on the sides to fold the book cover over the book. Then paint or draw Passover symbols and decorations on each cover: seder plate food, Elijah's wine glass, scenes from the story of the first Passover. Finish your book covers with sparkles, glitter, or sequins. You can even use your Haggadah covers as place cards, putting the name of each guest on a cover.

Blessing Wine

Here are the words to one of the important blessings at the seder:

Baruch Atta Adonai Eloheynu Melech Ha-Olam
Borey P'ri Ha-Gafen. Amen.

Praise be to God, King of the Universe,
Who creates the fruit of the vine. Amen.